what nature

poems

# what nature

STEVE FAY

TRIQUARTERLY BOOKS
NORTHWESTERN UNIVERSITY PRESS

Evanston, Illinois

TriQuarterly Books
Northwestern University Press
Evanston, Illinois 60208-4210

Printed in the United States of America

ISBN 0-8101-5078-6 (cloth)
ISBN 0-8101-5079-4 (paper)

Library of Congress Cataloging-in-Publication Data

Fay, Steve.
    What nature : poems / Steve Fay.
        p.  cm.
    Includes bibliographical references (p. )
    ISBN 0-8101-5078-6 (cloth : alk. paper). — ISBN 0-8101-5079-4 (paper :
    alk. paper)
        I. Man—Influence on nature—Middle West—Poetry. 2. Landscape—
    Middle West—Poetry. 3. Nature—Poetry. I. Title.
    PS3556.A9946W48 1998
    811'.54—dc21                                                      98-12692
                                                                        CIP

# contents

# acknowledgments

I am very grateful to the editors of the following publications in which the works listed below first appeared, sometimes in a different form or under a different title:

"Basco C. Adams Crosses the Bottoms Near Beardstown" in *Pudding.*
"Chemistry of the Prairie State" in *Northeast.*
"Crossings" in *Ascent.*
"The Firebird Diary" as "The Book of Lowilva: The Sister's Journal" in
    *Spoon River Poetry Review.*
"From a Handbook to Nature" in *Spoon River Quarterly.*
"Girl with Catfish" in *Illinois Review.*
"*Ictalurus*" in *Beloit Poetry Journal.*
"Intimacy Lessons" in *Newsletter Inago,* and subsequently in the anthology
    *TriQuarterly New Writers,* published by TriQuarterly Books/
    Northwestern University Press.
"Landscape" in *Rhetoric Review.*
"Lowilva Letters" in the anthology *TriQuarterly New Writers.*
"The Milkweed Parables" in *TriQuarterly,* and subsequently in the
    anthology *TriQuarterly New Writers.*
"The President Fishes from His Speedboat" in *Mississippi Valley Review.*
"Science" in *Snail's Pace Review.*
"Testament of Arkey Wilson" in *TriQuarterly.*

I would also like to thank the Illinois Arts Council for presenting me with a 1994 Literary Award and monetary prize for the poem "The Milkweed Parables" and a 1996 Special Assistance Grant in support of the production of an audio recording of "The Milkweed Parables."

what nature

I want to go a long way
where I will find myself
not as in a mirror
but as that other man who comes
from the other side of time

— John Knoepfle,
from *A Box of Sandalwood*

one

## Girl with Catfish

She is waiting below the barn, calling from the pig-tracked
   margin of the spring pond,
                    and also in faded snapshots
     curled where cellophane tape has given way
       from the barber shop wall,
                 and here as well in this
week's *Cuba Journal*, her prize beside her in front
   of the newly painted shed door;
                the fish's head as wide
   as her face, its body longer than her arm,
    she smiles that no one
           helped her pull it in.
And though it doesn't say, we know she must have impaled
   her own night crawler,
           tightening her lips intently,
   or because it says Spoon River, she may have hogged it,
    wading
        among rocks below Bernadotte Dam,

                  plunging
her fist into algal clefts until she was
   up to her elbow in barbeled flesh,
           risking Jonah's
   fate, yet landing her whale without being spat out.
   How the shadow of her jaw

            reminds of young Eve
plaiting verdant blades of savanna, daydreaming
   herself queen of the vast tribe
           called Wanderer.
   And here she waits behind the barn,
           below the creek bluff,

    manure-rich clay
drying on her Levis, her catfish gaping, surprised
    by sun and the locust-dry air.

# Landscape

*after John White's* Indians Fishing, *c. 1585*

There were never such fishers in Galilee,
                                        blessed
        without nets, raking
                            the hammerheads
            into their boat or waiting
                                    for the bonita to fly
to meet their spears.
                    *They are untroubled*
        *by desire*

                    *to pile up riches* wrote the Englishman
            while his painter-friend,
                                    mixing too much red
for the cooking fire laid mid-*cannow,*
                                confounded
        all perspective
                    with one
                            terrestrial cardinal flower
        rising

from that Virginia riverbed
                        —that green
mud on which the viewer,
                        extending lines, must stand
        thinking *shores of history,*
                        but slowly,
            slowly drowning.

# Science

Science is the tables of the powers of ten;
not really. It is the arithmetic in the water

budget sometimes. Really, you are out
on the prairie, following the dog's nose,

crisscrossing through the tall grass.
If you are lucky, you flush the cock pheasant,

and like a firecracker you go to heaven.
In Germany, Einstein couldn't get off

a clear shot. Someone took this photo of him
opening the door to his house,

muddy, his feet soaked,
a few beggar-ticks clinging to his sleeve.

## From a Handbook to Nature

We think the halls
of our arteries are dark:
we forget the fire

that burns at the tip
of each capillary.
It is the white

juice of the blood
burning there. That part
is really plant.

It is the reason
a man, on the coldest day
of his life,

wants to lie down
and sleep
with weeds under the snow,

expressing nothing.

10

# The Serpent's Complaint

*the chief sound of life is a hiss*
— Melville at Galapagos


Imagine your Eden pierced
                    by babble,
    Eve's rowdy kids stealing the iguana's eggs.
        Who wouldn't invent the Talking God to quell
such sacrilege?
                    Anything to get them off
    your island.
                    It had been quiet once,
        you mused—the slow pulse
                            of surf, gray
manna of lichen
                    growing on rocks of the caldera.
    What happened to the neighborhood?
                                    Still,
        the surf provides . . . all you had to say
was that the red coconut .
                    was *forbidden*
    and the bipeds—always suckers for a shell game—
        got drunk on milk, slew a child, and fled
like thieves on flimsy rafts.
                    How
                            could you have known
    they'd beget bikers
        wearing chains to haul
            your slow cousins off for soup tureens—
sporting
                their claws on cheap plated buckles?
    But it was when
                    the syllables of their canons
        more raucous than gulls
                            violated the bed
of the very sea,
                    you were finally convinced
    the Silent God
                    was dead.

11

## *Ictalurus*

When they built the Burlington Bridge, years ago,
they caught one on a crane hook that was so big
everybody thought it was a sunk log. Weighed
two full tons. They had to cut the cable because
it wasn't any use trying to get the hook back.

They were going to cut it for steaks at the sawmill,
but it was too tough for dog food. Some big-timer
bought it all up and ground fertilizer out of the meat,
carved walking sticks and gun stocks from the ribs,
and sold the skull to a museum in New York City.

I heard once that there's a fancy house in Spring-
field with a big window cut from that same old cat's
blue tailfin, but I don't expect that's true.

# Chemistry of the Prairie State

Ask for a bowl of chili
and a toasted cheese sandwich in
any bus station in Illinois and
it will taste the same; some
things are constants. Others are elements.

Twelve years ago at a building
site in Peoria, two boulders were
unearthed; when split open, one contained
a lost shipment of yellow and
green Dekalb Corn seed caps, the other
an antler plow and petrified corn.

Often discoveries like this are hushed
up by experienced contractors who know
that much hidden under dark loam
is better left buried; once near
Decatur, a vein of Sauk knives
and fertility dances was accidentally
uncovered by a farmer, resulting in
thirty-two hasty marriages and one death.

What is generally forgotten, however, is
the power of water to dissolve everything
living underground. Analysis of half-mile-deep
wells in Monmouth, and the Bell-Smith
Springs, reveals traces of kinnikinnick and
fox paw, German muscles and sow's
blood, Vachel Lindsay's tears to God.

Near Kellerville, especially, families attribute
miracles of healing and long life to

a daily consumption of these waters.
Always by the well, a tin cup
on a hook of wire, twisted
around the hands of the grandfather.

# The President
# Fishes from His Speedboat

*(1991)*

And because it would not be fitting
for him to weep openly for hostage or Kurd,
he takes himself away from shore
to bathe cut herring in the Atlantic of his heart.

There, off Maine, none
but the sworn agents of his secret service
shall glimpse the foundering of our ship of state,
and, soon, they turn away esteeming the sacrifice
   —to be presidential.

Though the great heart trembles,
he touches the throttles for our sakes
should skiffs with cameras near:
penants snap to, the president doffs his cap and
   smiles.

Lo, along riverbanks of cities and towns,
far inland, men and women
perish in the great boat's wake.

15

two

# The Milkweed Parables

*We bear the seeds of our return forever,*
*the flowers of our leaving, fruit of flight . . .*
— Muriel Rukeyser

## I. The Keeper

### 1

The girl saw something like it in the eyes of the men as they discussed how best to stack straw or butcher hogs.

Silently stirring the lard kettle with the heavy paddle, she would watch them argue about seasoning the sausage, then later, alone in the woods, try to wrinkle her nose like Augie Ochslein as if to interrupt her uncle, *Nein— Kein garlic! Oskar, du weisst—no garlic in mine.*

The others would laugh at him, but Mr. Ochslein clearly took pride in being the most persnickety neighbor.

Turning over leaves to find the new ginger shoots, she knew no adult would have appreciated such a finickiness in her, unless it was applied to swishing the bluebottles away from the cooling mincemeat pies.

So her vision grew in her eyes and her fingertips, and was called out at evening when the crows gathered along the opposite bluff of the creek.

And she said to no one but herself, *Tomorrow the hickory buds will open their small hands and call down rain.*

### 2

A demon of willfulness had once almost come to life before her in the coal-oil flicker of the parlor, as her uncle read in the almanac the story of a young girl struck down and disgraced by adventure.

And so she had willingly memorized the verses from the German Bible, and stayed away for a month from the catfish hole in the creek and fenceposts

and other places where it would have been easy for the Devil to reach up
from Hell and grab her.

But even then, she knew that she was drawn to another side, though she
did not know what was there.

Even her breathing became less girl-like at age twelve, with her turning to
walk up the small twisting draws from McGee Creek, watching the
growth of the gooseberry leaves, the sprouting acorns where a tree had
fallen, arriving home from school so late they assumed she had visited
Elsbeth.

And so she said she did and made up a story of what the old midwife had
asked, something about her boy, Oskar, that made her uncle shift, then
smile and forget about more scolding.

She only visited Elsbeth that next week to try to get her to talk about the
same things she herself had told, so that the old woman might later
remember and reply about such a visit from the girl once that spring.

She had never gone into the house of a woman who lived alone before, a
house with no man and a messy table, and everywhere small piles of
leaves and bark and paper.

As she followed hunched Elsbeth into the kitchen, she bumped her head
on a low-hanging shock of herbs, and white-plumed seeds fell from nar-
row pods catching like snowflakes in her auburn hair.

Elsbeth laughed and told her about curing Uncle Oskar of pleurisy with
the root of that same plant, as they drank sassafras tea and the girl only
played at removing the seeds from her hair, admiring the way they glis-
tened there with Elsbeth's small looking glass.

3

Thus one called may find a mentor.

But there was only that one summer, after she had turned twelve, when she
lived with and worked for Elsbeth, as they both told her mother and
uncle, Elsbeth paying for the girl's *housekeeping* with paper bundles of
cures and a mixture for brewing tonic for Oskar's mare.

It meant something coming in and nothing more going out to the school
next fall, except for Cousin Gus, Oskar's boy; it meant a *hardworking*,
more marriageable daughter for her mother.

But for herself, it meant finding Elsbeth's light in her own hands, feeling

the difference between poison and cure, as if in the dark, for it was sure-
ly darkness that hid this light from others.

It meant knowing, as surely as knowing straw, or butchering, or burning
brick or charcoal, and it meant laughing out loud sitting at the dirty
table with Elsbeth or calling in the crows together from the shade of the
hickory grove.

When Elsbeth caught the palsy in October's early freeze and could not tell
her what herbs to brew, she tried to find them on her own, but Elsbeth
was taken in a wagon to town and died.

She never knew if she could have saved her.

No one held her responsible, but they interrogated her, asking why she
wanted to keep living in Elsbeth's cluttered house, and for that matter,
*how had* she spent her housekeeper's time if the old woman's place was
such a sty.

In less than a month, as Uncle Oskar returned to supper sweaty and ner-
vous, her mother muttered, *Fertig—Ganz fertig—Ende,* and a fragrant
smoke twisted above the hickories as Elsbeth's herb stores burned.

The girl took up reading Psalms aloud each Sunday night and the ques-
tions stopped.

But when Gus choked on a fish bone, the week before Christmas, and she
made him swallow bread, as anyone but a child knew to do, Uncle
Oskar blurted that God be praised that she had stayed with Elsbeth, but
then he glanced to heaven and down again as if embarrassed and quick-
ly went to see about the calf.

Surely, the calf's small nose knew more about the light in yarrow and in
chicory and in maple twigs than her uncle, she thought, but he believed
his darkness was the light.

4

She learned to avert her eyes so that the others would not be troubled by
what showed through, and so she grew to adulthood in two worlds,
marrying Arnie Ochslein to please her mother, who was ill, and moving
back home to have her child when Arnie was hospitalized with malaria
in Manila, where he was soldiering.

The influenza took her mother before the cancer and she passed away in
spring.

And when the government telegram came about Arnie, Uncle Oskar pledged they would raise her baby as Gus's little brother, while large tears streamed down both sides of his furrowed nose.

Sunday afternoons that summer, when Gus had taken the wagon to his friend's and when her Uncle Oskar napped as if beneath the safe canopy of his pork-chop dinner, she would carry her baby out across the farm, through the hickories and along the creek, the small boy's hands mimicking her own as she reached to touch the leaves or as she knelt to touch the water.

If she handed him a stalk of goatsbeard, he stared transfixed, and he screamed beyond all decorum with delight when she blew away the buoyant seeds.

And the wordless baby, like his mother, hid all trace of these discoveries from the world of Oskar and Gus, kept it wrapped within the pod of his small secret soul.

5

That Monday in September, she hadn't known the cow had gotten down into the west ravine where the white snakeroot grows; Oskar hadn't told her.

But when the new milk smelled strange, she had thought better to drink a little of it herself to test it before giving it to her child, and when it did not seem so bad, she drank a bit more.

By the time Oskar ran in to say that cow had trembles, the milksickness had already begun to double her over.

As she lay on the kitchen floor, she thought she saw her son growing into a boy; could that be him coming in with the doctor, she wondered.

But it was Gus.

*The delirium's taking her . . . ,* the doctor's words floated apart from his bobbing face in the misty kitchen, . . . *the coma's next . . . takes a poison to fight a poison . . . arsenic . . . back, lad, . . . enough to kill a horse. . . .*

She fought the pill, trying to push from deep within, as if she were again giving birth, but the last push seemed to heave her clear, beyond and

above the house, far above poor Uncle Oskar rocking a baby in his arms
and standing beside the doctor's carriage.

Her hands reaching at last into the top of the hickory grove, now she could
count the weight of the kernels ripening before the frost.
She could hear the crows calling from the horizon, the echo of Elsbeth's
laugh.
Far on the other knoll, across the creek, they seemed to be covering some-
thing—baskets of new potatoes, she thought—in the kitchen of a farm-
house; a black carriage drove away, splashed through the ford, then
kicked a small curl of yellow dust above the bramble patch at the turn
toward town.

## II. The Flyer

I

In the black pool of McGee Creek, he touched his face, and it dissolved in
rings of light.
That game might have been at his young mother's urging, but he had long
abandoned such play when already the hired blade of the dozer severed
the meanders wreathing his lowland, to shunt the current down a
straight trough along the eastern boundary of the farm.
And after the willows had been smacked smooth, as he had heard the pio-
neers called it, and the old way of the creek graded level, each corner of
the new field lay quietly in the sun.

There was a year of gigantic corn.
But that triumph seemed a cheating when the next year floods rotted the
seeds, and the third autumn brought hail just before the harvest.
He might not have cursed the roping clouds that day had he known of the
coming decade of dust, years when the seedlings shot up as if to make a
bounty, only to wither by July.

At first he blamed the insidious milkweeds that also claimed his field of sun.
For weeks he patrolled the furrows with his hoe, striking off their milky

heads, but still they rose by the thousands above the dying corn, their
  seeds wrapped like snake-scales within the ovarian pods.
By November, their white hair shaken dry, they rose like a mist above the
  bottomland with every breeze rattling the frayed corn.
It seemed that the channel he had made worked too well, cutting fast and
  deep, drawing down the watertable as quickly as the earth along the
  gully fell away from the foot of his corner post.
Only stapled wire held him when the war came, and he was not as sorry as
  some others for his calling up.


2

In every way, the training suited him.
His carbine seemed much lighter than the hoe, and his field pack weighed
  no more from season to season.
He became a navigator in the Air Corps and watched the earth fall away
  farther and farther beneath his straightedge and protractor, triangles
  gathering fields, woods, and seas.
On his vellum charts, Normandy itself looked no bigger than his farm, and
  the shadow of the bomber stirred glimmers on the Channel effortlessly
  as a child's hand swishing in a bucket, or a creek.

He felt blessed when his parachute opened out of the choking, black
  smoke of the plane.
But soon after the crash, clouds gathering from the North Atlantic
  obscured his bobbing face from the other flights he heard passing home-
  ward overhead.
He cut the lines away but tried to keep one billow of the floating chute
  around his legs, in hopes it might hold a day's warmth within its white
  folds, as night came on.
Suspended among the swells in his life preserver, he dreamt of tropic bays
  and jellyfish dangling their tentacles, always with a cold sloshing at his ear.

## 3

Long after he stopped hearing the water, a voice came through static to enter his dream.

At times, it seemed as near and unending as his own slow but continuing breaths, unspooling through a modulation of grays he later guessed were days and nights.

The voice carried news of the war, invasions and lines held, but he tried to fix his mind on the smallest triumphs—a shepherd far to the north rescued by his dog from beneath an unexploded bomb—and the stories of human ingenuity that flow out of war.

A bounty, the voice told him, had been placed on the hollow hairs of milkweed, which could substitute in flotation vests for kapok fibers, now in short supply.

Children, let out of school in Canada, would collect carloads of the ripening pods for shipment to factories in Ohio.

A fever came on, or so he later believed, but at the time he knew only that the space beneath his eyelids blazed up white.

He felt the bed drift away and the weight of his body fall again into the webbing of the harness looped at his crotch.

His head jerked sideways as the chute canted above him in the crossways gusts.

He had been walking a long time, carrying the crumpled silk, following a furrow, marveling at its straightness and the fine texture of the clods drying brown along its ridge, when they took his arms and turned him around, bringing him into a corridor of brethren in white robes, dragging bandages.

He saw now that they had pulled him out of his coma and back into a world populated with human figures.

But when he tried to converse, the nurses only stared at his mouth, or nodded to one another, mumbling babble.

And his own voice dropped away when they led him to a mirror, and he
saw, looking up from the comb placed in his hand, his hair disheveled,
gone totally white.


4

The ocean voyage, the bus trip, the VA hospital—the days ran together.
He longed to hear the confident voice of the war, rasping its reports of tri-
umph.
He mused about his ancient bottomland field, the certainty of his plans,
the care of their execution, the first year's bounty of corn.
When he awoke in the home, gazing through solarium windows across a
broad creek valley, he believed for a moment his own will had trans-
ported him there.

Now even the seasons seemed to stream over him, the time punctuated
only by the recurrent visits of a young hazel-eyed girl—a sister's child he
told himself, though he remembered no sister, or a cousin's, if they had
returned him to Mount Sterling.
The youngster became one known face in a room of empty stares, and
what he liked best was that she never tried to make him speak.
Instead, the child would carefully turn his chair at evening so he could
watch the sun light up the serpentine coils of the creek lying on the far
side of the valley.
She seemed to detect in his eyes how this sight engaged him.

One evening, as the glint had just left the meanders and while the salmon
gold was fast receding on the trace of cirrus, he glanced down to dis-
cover his niece, as he had come to think of her, taking his left hand qui-
etly in her own.
The more to examine it than to show some pointless tenderness they were
both beyond, he adjudged looking on; *how they had become such idle
curiosities for one another.*

But as he watched, the dry flesh across his palm began to split, falling open
at her touch.
Dozens of small umber faces, wonderments trailing plumes of white hair,
began erupting from his lifeline.

Soon hundreds floated by their hair in the space around him.
Thousands obscured the child, the sun.

He felt his body lighten among them, as if he were adrift in the endless
white of a cool sea.

## III. The Passenger

I

Riding the train from Hyde Park, the cool morning of her fiftieth birth-
day, she had imagined becoming one of the museum's docents leading
schoolkids through the cultural exhibits, but as her group turned
through a musty granite arch, they would suddenly be outdoors, the
children turned into Potowatamis in black blankets welcoming Du
Sable—and behind a hut, where pumpkins were being cut into rings for
drying, a crowd of Hungarian stockyard workers with their *women and
children and a keg of beer and an accordion.*
The train itself, then, emerged from a tunnel onto a crescent mound of
glacial moraine, passing ice blocks studded with corpuscles of granite
from the Canadian Shield, each bobbing gently in one of the prairie
potholes dotting the flats that seemed to reach southwest all the way to
Blue Island, where the train slowed and an interesting-looking man she
thought she had noticed on the train another morning waved to her
from a wetland, mouthed *Hi, Honey,* yanked the cord of his gasoline-
powered trimmer, and roared a swath through the swamp milkweeds.

On such days, when the train was quiet, each passenger as lulled or as con-
voluted as she, she could lose track of her own state of wakefulness, the
city streaming by, itself a dream, the conductor's voice calling stops from
the mouth of a triumphant statue in Grant Park, his gray index finger
raised amid the pink branches of trees, calling, calling to each fellow
traveler.

It was just such a hand, monumentally old, that came and went in her
night dreams and nightsweats, though not a hand upraised in triumph,

but one curled down like an old root, the gray blanket, at first beneath it, changing to tan clay, like the soil under her own tiny fingernails, her own hand suddenly shrunken, pale, dimpled over the knuckles, a child's.

There would always be the shadow of a benign face, which moments earlier had drawn her near, yet always her gaze would seize upon the leathered knuckles, and she would reach out to them, taking them up mildly, as if unafraid, while elsewhere deep within her frozen body knowledge of the impending destroyer's clasp hovered and churned, dashing sour the warm milk she had sipped in vain.

There was never any avoiding of her dark fate.

It formed the very procession of her nights since childhood, and with every reaching she again became a child, open-eyed, innocently placing her hand into the trap of flesh, silent, warmed as if by unseen rays, loved even, until she tried to pull back.

The train was safer rest, she even took it on her day off, it was just the vehicle for the urban botanist, just the thing to break the spell of the museum's dessicated herbarium pages, cabinets of leaves and bark and paper.

True, she had no alternative; her only other wheels, the 1939 Ford 9-N tractor her father had purchased the day she was born, now rusted, some two hundred miles away, in a tumbled-down shed near McGee Creek, preserved for her in its natural coating of bird guano by the neighbor who bought the old home place years ago.

Unlike this birthright, the train never gathered dust; a silo of diversity it rolled onward as surely as the purple loosestrife overtaking the wild onions in the ditch just west of the tracks.

2

What she liked best about working on her day off was the relaxation, the freedom to return to her favorite specimens of the *Asclepiadaceae:* the wax plant, the tropical carrion flower, and the native butterfly weed— orangest orange of the Illinois prairies.

As self-appointed volunteer-for-a-day, she could not be rushed or prodded. *Back off, or I'll go home,* she once told a supervisor, and Ed, her friend, the black graphic artist, could hardly hold back his laughter—Ed, who loved the city enough to curse its inconsistencies; Ed, who could never understand the ones in her.

She had tried to make him see, the day he introduced her to fried egg-on-a-bagel; she had tried to explain how the city, the suburbs, everything northeast of Joliet had all been *the Rat Race* in the language of her home near Stickney, where her family had moved in her childhood, her father, a little old for World War Two, finding his duty and dollars greener than corn as a worker in the Chicago-area defense plants.

Real home was the eroded, tan banks of McGee Creek; she had learned to say *creek*, not *crick*, and *w-AH-sh*, not *worsh*, in the suburban kindergarten.

*Do you mean Honkies have to learn to talk that way, to get respect, just like Black Folks?* Ed inquired.

*Eloise, you're just a victim of white-on-white racism; they'll be making you move into my neighborhood next if you don't watch how you talk.*

From his baritone laugh and his nudging of her elbow to try another bit of the bagel, she knew he had meant no insult, more a trust, still she felt her love for him, like the failed fantasies of past loves, withdraw inside her like a small hand, the hand of a child, eager, yet afraid of unspoken punishment.

She wouldn't soon open her heart to him so much again.

At work, she and Ed were still *co-conspirators,* as he referred to them, with her drafting plans and text for new botanical exhibits, and him turning her notes and sketches into artwork for interpretive signs and display-case backgrounds.

And today, feeling more cheered than usual as she cleared things from her lab table, she discovered a note—in Ed's clear draftsman's hand—attached to a parcel: *Air Corps flotation vest: verify not filled with "weeds"—Military Museum.*

*Weeds? The army is afraid of weeds?*

As she unwrapped the faded yellow contraption, unclipping a rusty D-ring, a dose of mildew spores rose from the speckled canvas.

Wrinkling her nose, and trying not to breathe them in, she turned up a seam, and began to pick at the threads with her dissection probe and scalpel.

As each thread snapped, threads as old as she, the point of the blade rasped musically on the rough cloth.

Soon the handwork began to soothe her, letting her hum her way back again into thought, into childhood.

Calmly now, she realized there never had been a time when she had been at home; on the trips to visit her country cousins, she had never been one of them: she got into fights.

The closest connection came the autumn she turned seven, when her father was laid off from the plant for a time and they had stayed on her uncle's farm.

The uncle, really her father's second cousin, hadn't lived on the farm since before the war, had been shot down over the Channel, shocked into silence, withering like a cabbage in the nursing home window—surely no one to display alongside the sabers at the military museum.

She recalled his wavering slate eyes and white-ash hair.

With the tip of her forceps, she withdrew a bright, downy structure from the vest's crumbly interior.

*Milkweed coma*, she said, raising the specimen up to Ed, who had just returned with a cup of coffee.

*I knew you'd know!* he exhaled over the brew; *may as well throw it out, though; they don't want to know the truth about weeds.*

She couldn't help smiling, wondering at Ed's faith in her and at her own knack for taxonomy—where had it come from?

Her uncle's mother, it had been said, was a bit of an herbalist, but not a great one, having died of milksickness like Lincoln's mother.

3

She placed the delicate white strands under the microscope and focused.

A small dark fleck that had looked like a granule of soil at first resolved into a short, barbed shaft—a bit of insect foot.

But then, seemingly without her adjustment of the wheel, the image suddenly blurred, distorting as it did into something gripping, shriveled, branching down.

She shuddered back into the cold backrest of her stool.

What had she seen, or felt?

It had almost been as if something inside her, some pattern long preserved in the onyx tree of her spine, had deformed like magma in the focused beam above the lens.

Gritting her teeth, she brought her left eye back to the scope, reminding herself to keep her right eye open.

With her fingertips, she adjusted the aperture below the microscope stage—no mistake now.

Here it was, clear this time, the gnarled, remnant clasp from a pollinium, the saddlebag of pollen that the milkweed shackles onto unwary travelers.

She breathed in, exhaling slowly to steady herself.

She imagined the Lilliputian drama, the small wasp kindly caressing the five-part flower, mild glee, or whatever passes for insect warmth, filling its thorax, until the fateful misstep.

How long did it buzz its voiceless scream before tearing free (or was it able)?

And even then, no complete freedom, still carrying the microbial baggage around for how many flights over the meadow, before finally implanting it in another flower, perhaps only to get trapped once more.

Bees have been found with more than twenty of these dried souvenirs on their limbs, fated for capture again and again, vectors for designs beyond their ken.

How strange to find the ephemeral flower-part among the chaff of long-harvested fruits.

*You say it's mine if I want it?*

Ed nodded.

*Let's cross over to the lake, then, by the Aquarium, and see if it still floats.*

Sitting along the breakwater, tying an umbilical of twine through the D-ring of the ancient life preserver, which she had hastily stapled back together, she felt warmed by Ed's readiness to go along on their military field test.

He cheered her lariat-style launching of the yellow bundle and its splash onto the green swells, where it bobbed and surged.

They sat a long while silently watching the vest, listening to the faint voices that rode the wind from offshore boats, miraculously pushing back the traffic noise only yards behind them.

*My uncle was saved by one of these things—in the war,* she said finally.

*What happened to him after that?*

*They told me he died in the nursing home; I used to visit him when I was a kid.*

They both looked out again into the blue distances of the lake.

Is gazing in parallel looking away? she wondered.

She could hear the breeze tapping Ed's shirtsleeve just above his burnt-umber elbow.

Far out, she could see how the waves made band after precise band of blue-gray and white, as if they were furrows freshly plowed by the coal ship now threading the horizon.

Focusing her eyes more closely on the lines of waves, she imagined what it would be like to float for hours or days among them.

While she kept watch, the silvery ridges began to look increasingly like the rails of the vast freight yard of a vaster, but invisible Chicago, and as the plane of the yard gradually tipped up closer, it became a striated wall of ice, preparing to raze the knolls of Illinois once more.

three

# Intimacy Lessons

### 1

Above green grass clumps, coarse rusted wire,
bent steel fenceposts, and heaped dirt, raspberry
vines curl stickery out of the windshield hole
of the dented hulk of a forties' Plymouth.
I hear the fearful springs of our father's
nineteen fifty-five Pontiac splashing
through the puddled ruts of winter.

### 2

Now is the time when the spiny frost begins
to melt off the tattered leaves of the curly dock.
By six-thirty, it will all be gone.
Is the leaf turned on edge? I am too close to see
except for faint rose veins over pale green ice.
Just now, my feet slip toward the white depth.

### 3

This pink rind of the year suspends all belief.
Starvation isn't working; only my will
gets thinner. The bird just under my breastbone,
tries to get out, eats the suet from my ribs.

### 4

I dreamt the reoccurring dream again and waited
by the pond to find its heat. In the dream, when
the damselflies stirred the frogs, I followed
the cowtrail through the grass to the opened
three-wire gate. I looked for the grass
that sprang instant from the broadcast seeds,
the square I scythed in the flowering spurge.

5

High water and wind blowing, low to the ground,
zinging through the hazel bushes, roiling over
fences, snapping cottonwood boughs, left a poplar
feather-like on the billboard for Maquon.
A broken cloud voice, the child in the green dress
weaves herself a headdress of red sumac leaves.


6

Many dawns pass unnoticed, but not this stroke
of orange on a stony range of clouds.
Once I ran from a cold tent to catch the sunrise
above Forbes Lake; the sun, forgetting
the height of the trees, was an hour late.

7

The turbid pool gnaws the coffee-colored bank,
What gems do you expect to find along
the sprawling hips of the Mississippi? God,
the bullhead swimming among dark willow roots!
I have started toward a shrine of sticks and mud,
the way toward tangle, where it all connects
like a pencil sketch, retraced studies of a face,
where the cosmos will cup its hand over me.


8

As the deerfly wears the fawn's spots on her wings,
so, in the damp shadow of eyes, dim retinas
become aerial views of rivers, wingprints of
mourning cloak butterflies, fantastic migrations
of starfish, sapphire stars glowing in the blue corn.
Such are the moist-earthed intentions, the politics of
morels, the last flash of red in the fall apple
twigs, the fragrance of a lover's unpinned hair,
the sad lover, so surprised to give up doubts.

## Basco C. Adams
## Crosses the Bottoms Near Beardstown

*I*

A fall-tilled field, a red-tailed hawk,
and the sky opening up
as the van descended from the Rushville bluffs,
that's what I remember—nothing ordinary.

And now, after thirteen years,
this time a gale at my back,
and breakers of cloud rolling through the sky all day,

I cross the Beardstown bridge to find:
    egrets in a pool of sun, and ascending
    in a calm, above golden beans, above copper corn,
    the great blue heron.

*II*

Don't call me a romantic; I can see
the run-down towns, the subsoil sloshing in the spring creeks,
and the cowboys in Springfield.
I know my state is on the shoals.

But my mind keeps meandering toward a rocky beach
at another, or maybe this bridge,
where at four I was brought to touch
the Illinois River water.

And while no dove rose or fell to seal the sacrament,
it was witnessed by a string of corn and coal barges,
and benediction given by three jays on high
in a cottonwood.

And ever since, I'm set apart from other people in this one thing;
whether I walk, drive, or ride the Trailways bus,
I can never find a river on its day off—
there is always a show, quail-calling me back to this valley:
    to look for work in its slim newspapers,
    to read of a copycat Lysol suicide, like Vachel Lindsay's,
    and to try to look kindly
    into the strange eyes at auctions.

# Verschwistert

I test the small reddening seeds
to see if they are past their milk.
Sister, I take these tawny leaves
you loved into my fingers, gauge
their stems against the lines of my palm
for what remains of August softness.
The head-high plumes of Indian grass
turn ghostly, sway around me,
with me more and more lost
in the hidden tongue of the field.
Then your hand gestures, and I release
their feathered bronze with a touch,
bending to strip the lower spikes,
reaching up to pull the tallest ones
slowly against a thumbnail—and
all of this I felt inside me
days before this wading into sun.

2

I rattle the grocery bag among
the giant clumps of prairie
which sift dryly against my cuffs.
Then, with the bag half-filled,
I carry the seeds to the barren hayfield
and fling them onto the breeze
electric with locust song,
where they spark in the air
and fall into the dying alfalfa.
Once I thought we did all this
to preserve these feathered grasses,
but now I have to grip these kernels,

press them into my skin, know
the feel of their scatter.

I must lie among them in the stubble:
as the West goes pale,
silhouetting the green orbs that remain
where the black walnut has pawned
its leaves; as headless Orion,
the mantis, ascends the eastern sky,
and his red-eyed daughters climb
blades which curl down over me
to lay their silvered eggs.
My own dim cells would percolate
between these roots leaving nothing
but a ring of salt upon the clay, or badge
of lichen on a flat stone.

# Testament of Arkey Wilson

I wake at sunup with my feet pointed toward Arkansas.
I wonder if it was providence that the trailer was already turned that way
when me and Patsy bought it and moved our little daughters, Dolly and
  June, up from the floodplain,
our son, Cantrell Jr., already dead in prison, never learning to read even as
  good as me, getting fired from jobs Hank helped me help him get. *A
  bruised reed,*
*he ain't going to break,* Jesus preached, but Canny shot a cop who caught
  him smoking near drained Lima Lake.

The mouth of a gun,
the mouth of a boy who can't let on he can't read,
the mouth that gets you into trouble behind bars,
the mouth of his mother, my wife, hardly talking for a year after that.

And there was Hank, my friend, who hired me sometimes to help repair
  grain elevators with his crew,
or drive to Keokuk or Davenport for a part,
or even fix them sandwiches so he could slip me five bucks when I was let
  go from bartending—
Hank trying to raise those two kids *without* a wife,
  relying on half-crazy relatives scattered in a half-dozen little towns:
      Pontusuc, Keithsburg, Buffalo Prairie,
  and places like Shanghai that ain't even on a map.

And that day finding Hank collapsed one more time, an attack of the her-
  nia he wouldn't get help for,
lying there on the hardened, spilled tar behind his toolshed,

him reaching up to me,
saying, *Arkey, someday tell my kids . . .*
just before he passed out.

Just what to tell them, he didn't have to explain.
I knew he meant more than to straighten them out about some gossip on
    his family he guessed had got around to them,
he meant something about a father's guilt that he couldn't do better—what
    I wish
I could ask somebody else to say to mine, for me, but with Hank gone I
    got nobody to ask.

Oh, he didn't die then;

he finally had to get the operation,
lived the long life of the ornery, I used to say, for years after that.
But what I said to him *then,* sitting with him to wait for the ambulance,
noticing how even with his rough, work-dirty hands he looked like a worn-
    out kid finally taking his nap,
what I said was how Jesus said to *give the little children a cool drink of well-
    water.*

Not the water of the Mississippi, I thought,
remembering my own home along the delta, and what I'd seen
    of the fevered generations
    of this whole land.

four

# The Book of Lowilva

## *I. Lowilva letters*

1

To hover two fathoms above the knee-high corn is the feat
    of my dreams these June nights.
                                    You are there
        seated again beside me on the front seat of the Buick,
looking like the cover of the Penneys catalog, 1953.

    You unchanged, but I know the consequences, half of me
        surprised how calm we are, drenched in the cicada song
of our impromptu wings and the dank starlight of the floodplain,
    as if we both had meant to fly from the curve on the Levee Road.

    We never land in my dream, and the band of willows
which must have cartwheeled us into the drainage ditch
    is nothing but a glimmer in the headlights' farthest reach.

    I alone crash, as the glare of eyes touches off the dawn
of your blood on my palms, waking me to thunder without rain.

    And for the moment I'm convinced it is a message you have died
        in a distant state, some funeral home hairdresser brushing
back your hair to find what you have always hid, the white
        meandering trace across your forehead—my gift to you.

2

That day as children we climbed the river dunes
north of Oquawka—over and over, you always ahead
of me, the black Lab, Old Shirley, ahead of you.
You counted off each lap, I wheezed. The Lab
still ready to swim for the driftwood
we heaved into the channel, when I finally dropped
on the hot yellow sand, and you fell and kissed me.

We both were nine, both called the same man *Father*.
We had no name for who we were to each other, no name
for what we swam for, young retrievers caught in the current.

3

A man of thirty who pats his belly and talks cute
to sell the sponsor's milk to the kiddies
can be a hit on TV, but he's a joke back home.
Arkey set up those shots of milk when I went in for a beer,
so I ordered my whiskey by the bottle like the black hats
in those cut-rate Western serials I introduced. You finally
said, *Get out, damn you.* We might have lived on together
in Buffalo Prairie after Dad died, the two of us
a natural family. I can't go by the house now,
without thinking I've just missed you on the porch.

4

You said, *Illinois is pregnant!*
                              *Then who's*
*the father,* I quipped, *Indiana?*
                                        It was starting
even then. But mainly I hated you
wasting your time with that basketball player
when we could have driven to the river
in my Hudson. I told you he would dump you
when he got to college. And you were
never sorry, once we got there. As I brushed
the sand from my plate, you'd grab my face
in your hands, point my eyes up,
                              *Look, Stupid,*
*at the clouds breaking over the bluffs, they're*
*doing it again!* you'd say.
                              *They're only clouds!*
I had to say that then, but now, at fifty, I see
it all the time: the lines of surf
in a billowing arc across the sky, mimicking
the great western bulge of the Mississippi
like maternity wear for the state.

I have taken to walking in cemeteries, among the lost
stones, without promise of perpetual care.

They are more numerous than morels
waiting beneath rotted elm roots.

Pioneer settlers, infants lost to fever, families
cleaved by sleigh runners and spring floods.

I part a stand of big bluestem grass with my stick.
A marker appears, washed blank by a hundred years of rain.

I lift the small lichen-covered slab; words long dissolved
from the mud-stained side have left their imprint in the clay.

I trace them in reverse, close my eyes: *Beloved Sister.*

6

On my way to conduct the interview at the returning
astronaut's home, I wondered how I could rise above
the usual *hometown boy makes good* appeal. I was
on-task, professional down to my black shoes, dutiful
as my tape recorder, new batteries, tape already cued.

Then I saw *him* behind me in the rearview, him twenty
years dead, but driving a Ford through the middle
of Quincy—as if he were escorting me to work, worried
my alternator was going bad. Hardly looking ahead,
I studied the once-familiar hairline and twelve o'clock
shadow; only the ruby tip of his cigarette was absent.

Then I heard your voice, also years unknown, saying
*Our father,* softly, as when you played you were older.

7

What was our religion, anyway? Memory?
Penance? The family lore?
Or is that just another damnation?

What stories did we tell one another in our silences together?
I told you a story once that scared you away, west of the river,
     the *Firebird Country,* you called it.
Away from the family touch.
Away from my Jim Beam youth that almost killed you.

There is no one here for me now, for my old age.
I would write you that I have changed, that I ask and expect
nothing. But you won't answer; I have already written the
     answer on your flesh.

This is where our silence has taken us.
You are the pulling current in my blood, washing over
     the shoals I make
     of broken glass.

## II. The Firebird Diary

### 1. February

The calf outside the fence, the pasture alongside the highway.
I was passing by in the far lane, not speeding this time,

and shuddered my foot off the gas when her small face started
in my direction. There would be a truck soon barreling down

too near the calf, a grain truck or a delivery van, the driver
making up for lost time on his route. My pulse strayed

over the few feet of grass between the calf and the pavement.
But then I saw the farmer, moving quietly among small cedars

near the fencepost, there to protect his investment,
and the four other black-and-brown calves gathered near him

inside the fence. The farmer taking his hand from out
of a yellow chore glove, dragging his palm slowly against

the weave of the fence wire, fingers down like a small deformed
udder, a hopeless-looking sight—but the calf turned to it,

the pink and linty sign of mother, diminutive as it was,
and followed it in fascination, gradually gateward.

The gate was far.
                    The man, though irritated, behaved

with patience. I slowly pushed the accelerator down,
picked up speed, tried to look as if I had been concerned

only for my fuel injection. But in a few miles a virulence
overtook me. I pulled over near a roadside park. Wept.

Wept until . . . until I was silent. It was as if I had witnessed
my own life, my following or my straying from some image

of warmth, its truth taken away in my infancy; its false sign,
like the surrogate udder, all that was ever held out to me.

When I heard the crow starting to claim a line of Osage orange,
when I tried to unbend to look out across the pasture,

I found my arms crossed tightly—not reaching,
not reaching anywhere—clasped over my own breasts.

## 2. March

Where were we running with those strangely lit faces?
Playing tag with our father's friend's children, outside,

at night? Was it because their house smelled like methane?
Passing the dirty magazine pictures by flashlight,

their favorite pastime retrieved from under the pile of junk tires.
The show-butts game my brother asserted we didn't have to play.

I was too queasy, the electric flavor of dehydration
unswallowable on the back of my tongue. It is still too much

for me when I taste it again, noticing near dusk how elm twigs
pulse against spring's clouds. He, my brother, was offspring

of that same placental sky, though Aunt Meda, sipping
her Old Nauvoo wine, had let slip one time that he was no kin

to me—while somehow she had forgotten just which of us
had been the unfortunate bastard foundling. But, as they say,

when both sides of the ditch are on fire, it doesn't matter
who planted the grass.

                              I wouldn't want to see him now.
He's probably dead, or cold. But driving tonight, I thought I

saw his twelve-year-face, wizened as by a flashlight beam.
"Who were those boys who threw the cherry bombs down

the gopher homes?" I wanted to ask him; I could kill
them now. "Tell me, again, about our mother." Where did

he ever get those stories? Across the darkened bottomlands
of the Des Moines River, orange sickles sweep along the levees—

now's the season for plowing and pyromania in farm country.
But, as my brother taught me, it's a car crash that sometimes

sets these blazes. Whoever is pulled alive from that womb
of fire and glass is born an orphan. And an only child.

## 3. June

"Where were the June bugs?" I wondered in Colorado.
And, at the Great Sad Lake, "Had Brigham Young's teenaged brides

flown all this way, like the Mormonflies I saw, at their age,
billowing up from the Keokuk bluffs?" The fauna, the humans

were strange to me those first years in the West, and with
the mountains rising up like thunderheads along the horizon,

it always looked like rain. Until I learned that the bellies
of cloud had all been bruised dry by the white knuckles

of the Rockies. I don't know why, but the granite and snow
seemed so temporary to me, frail peaks like my string of jobs:

waitress, file clerk, community college instructor, waitress,
used car lot receptionist, telemarketeer, rodeo ticket-taker,

library assistant, manager trainee, motel night clerk,
tutor, volunteer, tourist, always, finally, tourist.

Then I came down to the Platte
                —river of eternal mud—

and found the migrations of sandhill cranes, squawking
and dancing for love as they'd done for ten thousand years,

and I set up my business—Used Books, Consignments,
Quilters' Supplies—that drew in hordes of great-grandmothers,

swarms of country dancers, and that one widower gesturing
louder than his parched words, leaving behind a carton

of his wife's bright pantsuits and sundresses.
And when the pharmacist and I walked along the river

in a balmy wind, and he said that the cottonwood seeds
were blowing clear to Illinois, it was the end of my flight,

and I bought a tiny house and visited a church,
and went on silly dates with him, which ended in his bed,

having found that strand of fertile mud, where the seed
may stick after blowing over miles of dry ground.

## 4. July

When I was married, it was one of those things of which
my husband silently disapproved: a photo of a woman

by a clapboard wall, a loop of thicket creeper above and behind
her shoulder. Twenty dollars *was* too much to spend

for the small, stained portrait, faded of sepia, with
the half-scuffed signature of an Omaha photographer.

"It was the fabric of her dress that made me buy it,"
I explained, repeating myself, a pattern I remembered

from odd pieces of an old family quilt.
                                        "A crazy quilt,"

he laughed, knowing them only from my stories; I never said
that it was the same cotton print I had made believe

my mother wore, or that this woman snapped in her thirties,
in *the* Thirties, had become Her in my imaginings from then on.

And now, with The Druggist long imagined out of my life,
I find the perfect oval frame, plain and worn, small as her,

not needing a custom-cut matboard in the analgesic blue
of bedroom curtains. And from that Ottumwa junk shop,

I drive three hours to Geode Park, sit as dusk rises from draws,
prying with my knife at the brads on the frame's back,

wiggling the photo into place, holding it out to make
adjustments, then bringing it finally back against

the darkness of my cheek.
                          Fifty miles east, and across

the Mississippi, I was raised, with a proxy brother,
among fat aunts and a grizzled father. Here, like there,

the coyote calls echo above the pin oak bottoms, then fade,
soften behind blackened ridges. An ex-naturalist in Colorado

told me that the lone animal's howl for the pack, its moan
for the round face of the moon, is Mammal for "Without."

## 5. September

At the filling station, the owner and the customer disagreed:
whether it had been Willa Cather or Laura Ingalls Wilder;

whether she had visited, attending a funeral, or was
buried there; whether her companion was friend or relation

and whether she had been Iowa's own Maud Bliss Camp
or Mrs. Orpha Klopfstein Grenier; whether Maud or Orpha was

the more underrated and unfairly forgotten poet; whether
it was the local Audubon Society or the Nature Conservancy

out of Des Moines that had pulled up the honeysuckle
and let the prairie weeds grow, whether it was Indian grass

or Johnson grass that was supposed to be so lush there;
whether it was best to go on following the state route

or to turn at the corner where the old schoolhouse used to be;
whether the bridge had washed out or was only covered

with gang graffiti.
                    I didn't ask: if it was mere coincidence

that the cemetery had the same name as an Illinois village
named for its mayor's prize rooster, where a circus elephant

struck by lightning had the largest headstone; where
my brother claimed, at different times, three locations

for our mother's body; where, once drunk, he told me
the joke about the Kiwanis Club's official condom;

where I looked again for her name among toppled, broken,
dissolving marble; where I plucked goldenrod till

my palms were yellow, before hitchhiking to Muscatine;
where the beggar-ticks caught my sleeve and rode hobo

that night on me, me as empty as a boxcar,
knocking my way west, after dry dust of the sun.

five

# Crossings

It crosses years,
it might as well be luggage for the DC-3 from Quincy

to St. Louis, a DC-3 from Havana to Miami, the flight plan
of the bobolink from Concord, Mass., to the Florida Keys

or the butterbird from the Keys to Jamaica, the map
the termite follows from soil to beam. The termite

crossing always inside, through the tunnel of the rafter,
the last train from Basco to Carthage, polishing the rails,

the image on the once-lost and now-found photograph,
the immigrant ancestor crossing from *Jannson* to *Johnson*.

My grandmother's hidden tin of *Heather, Soft, soft, red rouge,*
crossing her aged cheek, the knowledge of it

crossing, through an aunt's clutched fingers, wrapping it
in the note. The note, bottled up, as if it were crossing the ocean

to London, or the gulf between Moscow, Idaho, and Havana, Illinois.
Drifting past the islands off coasts, sticking to one thing,

like a postage stamp, until it gets there, the stamp
so enviable and tidy. The termite chewing the stamps

on the hidden war letters, tasting the flour of affection, the colony
of microflora crossing between paper fibers deep within

the termite's gut. The milkweed seed crossing the field,
the tornado crossing the trailer park, the wagon crossing

Cumberland Gap, Black Hawk's last crossing of the Mississippi
away from starvation and into massacre. The chair rocking

in the flatboat and later in the split-level house, the same
chair once hacked by a child's sharp hatchet,

as if it would serve as well to stew a chicken.
The crossing of the bullet from the marksman to the target,

from the mob into Elijah Lovejoy, the other mob
into the Mormon prophet. Capone's mob hunting ducks near Beardstown

with Thompson submachine guns. Captain Lincoln, who fired no shot
in the Black Hawk War, crossing the Illinois River in flood.

The flame crossing the vapor from the fuel tank, the life
crossing beneath the bandage, the unsent letter, never crossing

the continental divide. The stamp on the tongue
crossing to the envelope, the interrupted scrawl crossing

to the retina. The stamp on the heart, the termite
crossing within the beam, the blood in the artery crossing.

# notes

### Girl with Catfish

hogged        Hogging is a method of catching large catfish by hand, as practiced in the Spoon River.

Eve        Researchers into mitochondral DNA, passed matrilineally through the mother's egg cell, have hypothesized a literal Eve, mother of our species.

### *Ictalurus*

*Ictalurus*        Genus of U.S. freshwater catfishes and bullheads.

### Chemistry of the Prairie State

kinnikinnick        Native American smoking mixture, chiefly composed of tobacco while tribes still retained control of their fields and trade.

### The Milkweed Parables

pleurisy        The orange-flowered milkweed, *Asclepias tuberosa,* was formerly called "pleurisy root."

burning brick or charcoal    Local manufacture of building bricks and of charcoal.

*Fertig—Ganz fertig—Ende*    German for "Finished—done—the end."

white snakeroot        A fall-blooming plant of eastern forests, eventually discovered to be the cause of the disease trembles in livestock and the potentially fatal milksickness in humans.

coma        Latin for "hair," also, the tail of a comet and the silky tufts on some seeds.

Du Sable        Jean-Baptiste Point du Sable, a trader of African descent, probably born a slave in the Caribbean, who began the first permanent non-native settlement at Chicago by establishing a trading post in about 1779.

*women . . . accordion*    From Carl Sandburg's "Happiness," in *Chicago Poems.*

| | |
|---|---|
| wild onions | Or *place of the wild onions*, meaning of the Native American word(s) for which "Chicago" is thought to be a transliteration. |

## Verschwistert

| | |
|---|---|
| *verschwistert* | German, roughly meaning "besistered" (as in bewitched). |

## The Book of Lowilva

| | |
|---|---|
| Lowilva | Coined by archeaologist Stuart Streuver and Felicia Antonelli Holton to stand for *LO*-wer *IL*-linois *VA*-lley, used here for the entire region between the Illinois River and the Mississippi, south of the former trace of the Hennepin Canal. |
| bellies of cloud . . . bruised dry | Precipitation on the western slopes of the Rocky Mountains creates a rain shadow of dry air, which contributed to the origin of the nearly treeless prairies of the Great Plains and portions of the Midwest. |

## Crossings

| | |
|---|---|
| bobolink, butterbird | Different local names for the longest-migrating land bird of the Americas, which summers as far north as southeastern Canada and winters in the Chaco region of Argentina. |
| Black Hawk | An elderly head man of the Sauk village formerly located at the mouth of the Rock River on the Mississippi, Black [Sparrow] Hawk ordered white squatters who had destroyed his people's corn-fields to leave in the spring of 1831, but in the face of a rallying of 2500 troops, he reluctantly evacu-ated his people to Iowa. An avoidable and very disorganized war broke out the following spring when, after a failed winter hunt, Black Hawk brought 1500 of his people back to Illinois to make a corn crop. They were chased through much of northwestern Illinois and southern Wisconsin, until August of 1832, when the remaining Sauk people, most of them unarmed, were nearly wiped out trying to escape into the waters of the Mississippi (south of La Crosse, Wisconsin) while |

caught in a crossfire between troops on shore and an armed steamer on the river.

| | |
|---|---|
| **Elijah Lovejoy** | Abolitionist newspaper editor, assassinated while defending his press in Alton, Illinois, in 1837. |
| **Mormon prophet** | Joseph Smith, assassinated when a mob stormed the jail in Carthage, Illinois, where he was being held, in 1844, leading within two years to his people's abandonment of the quasi-city-state of Nauvoo, many of them fleeing over the frozen Mississippi, on their way to Utah. |
| **continental divide** | Including the divide between the Great Lakes–St. Lawrence River drainage basin and the Mississippi River drainage basin, which southwest of Chicago was only about four feet high. |